HAPPY CHRISTMAS
HAVE FUN & GREAT SEX !

Romantic Dinner...

Morning Sex...

Naked Chef...

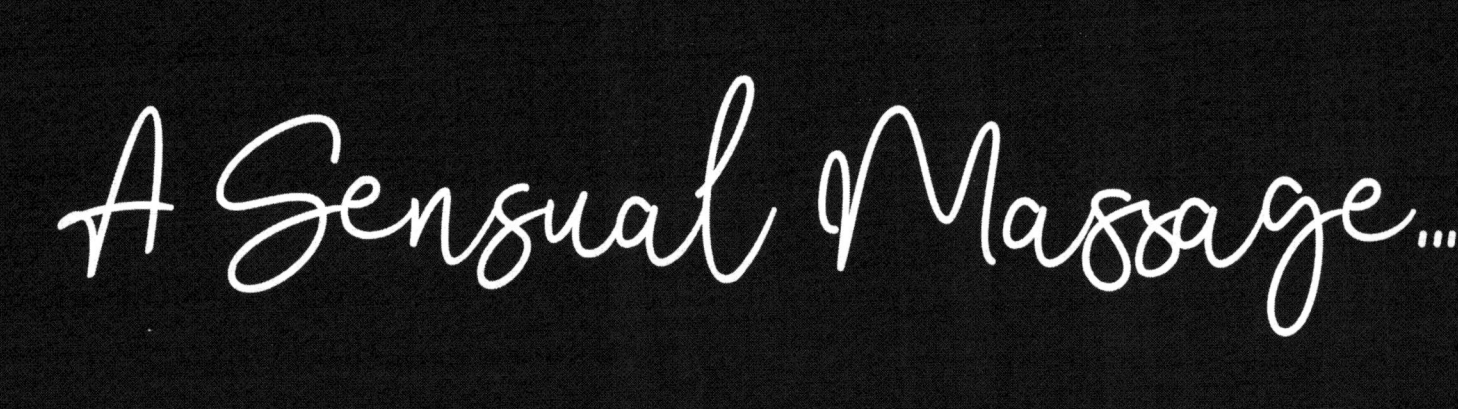

Tell Me Where You Want To Touch Me First...

Household Chore (Nude)...

A "Yes" Day...

Photoshoot...

It's Time For 69...

Sexy Spanks...

Undress Me With Your Teeth And...

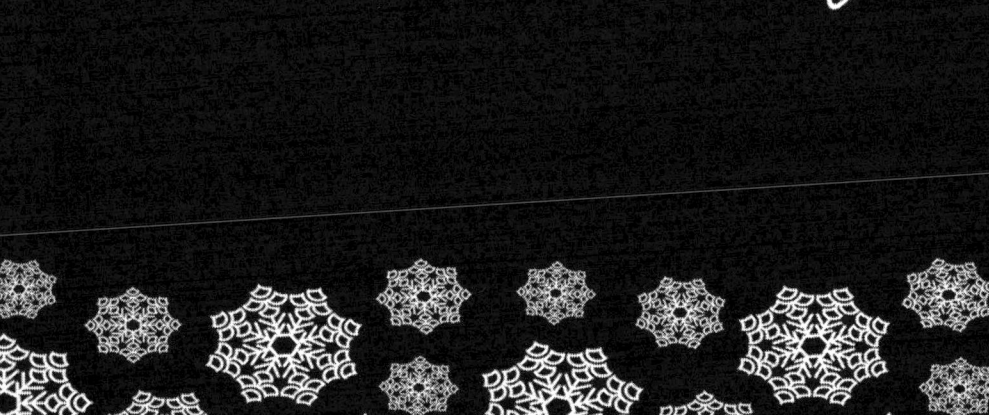

A Free Naughty Wish...

Strip Tease...

New Position...

No Panties Day...

Dirty Talk...

100 Kisses But Not On The Lips...

Bath For Two...

Game in Santa...

IF YOU WANT TO SEE MY LOVE
BOOKS, JUST SCAN THE QR CODE
WANT, YOU CAN LEAVE ME A REVIEW ON

Made in the USA
Las Vegas, NV
18 November 2022